Ice Cream Cakes

Simple, Delicious & Impressive Party-Perfect Cakes!

Printed in the United States of America
by G&R Publishing Co.

Published By:

507 Industrial Street
Waverly, IA 50677

ISBN-13: 978-1-56383-0
ISBN-10: 1-56383-338-7
Item #7037

Table of Contents

Getting Started...4
Simple Fudge Crunch Ice Cream Cake 8
Cake & Coffee Ice Cream Combo.....................10
Gingersnap Toffee Bombe.................................12
Crispy Peanut Butter-Chocolate Craving..........14
Chocolate Pretzel Deluxe..................................16
7-Layer Neapolitan Loaf....................................18
Banana Split Ice Cream Cake............................20
Chocolate & Orange Delight 22
Amaretto Angel Cake 24
Raspberry Creamsicle Cake 25
Layered Frozen Peach Cobbler...........................26
Macaroon Torte 28
Tic-Tac-Toe Fun 30
Raspberry Ribbon Beauty..................................32
Mexican Crunch Ice Cream Cake 34
Strawberry Jelly Roll Swirl.................................36
Mint Chip Chocolate Stack.................................38
Giant Brownie Ice Cream Sandwich 40
Chocolate Chunk Ice Cream Squares.................42
Sherbet & Ice Cream Party Cake.......................44
Frozen Black Forest Elegance 46
Strawberry & Brownie Bombe 48
Individual Baked Alaska 50
Chocolate Peppermint Cake Roll 52
Lemon Tunnel Surprise 54
Coconut Tunnel Surprise.....................................55
Quick & Elegant Ice Cream Sandwich Torte 56
Pumpkin-Chip S'mores 58
Tasty Combos 60

Getting Started

Ice cream cakes are beautiful to serve, yummy to eat and great for fix-ahead convenience. Though some require several stages of freezer time, once ice cream cakes are assembled and frozen, most can remain in the freezer for several weeks before serving. Simply remove them from the freezer, let soften slightly, cut and serve.

Use the recipes and techniques described here or create other tasty combinations with your favorite flavors of ice cream, sherbet, sorbet or frozen yogurt. Add layers of sponge cake, crushed cookies or sauces for a variety of textures and flavors. Cakes may be frosted with buttercream frosting, whipped cream, whipped topping or additional softened ice cream or sherbet. Add garnishes before freezing or just before serving.

The following hints and tips will help even the ice cream cake novice create beautiful and delicious masterpieces.

How to...

Soften ice cream: Place the package of ice cream in the refrigerator for 20 to 30 minutes, or let it stand at room temperature for 10 to 15 minutes until just soft enough to spread. You may also scoop the desired amount of ice cream into a large bowl, let it soften and then stir well with a large spoon or rubber scraper. Be sure to use the softened ice cream before it becomes soupy. If it gets too soft, return it to the freezer until it is firm enough to handle easily. In some recipes, it's easier to cut slices of ice cream while firm and then assemble the slices as directed. Open or cut off the cardboard carton to make uniform slices. Buy a half-gallon box to get rectangular slices; freeze any leftover ice cream for another use.

Wrap cakes for freezing: Cakes may be set inside an airtight plastic container and placed in the freezer. Cakes in pans can be covered tightly with plastic wrap or foil. Cakes without pans need support on the bottom, so set them on a freezer-safe plate, baking

4

sheet or sturdy piece of foil-wrapped cardboard and then wrap in foil to maintain the cake's shape.

Freeze ice cream cakes: Cakes must be frozen for a minimum of 2 to 3 hours to harden, depending on freezer temperature. Most can be frozen overnight or for several weeks with good results if wrapped well. Be sure cakes sit on a level surface in the freezer.

Remove a whole cake (or cake layer) from its pan:

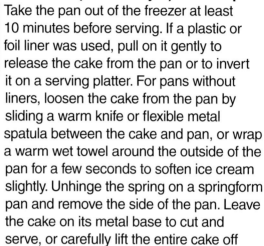

Take the pan out of the freezer at least 10 minutes before serving. If a plastic or foil liner was used, pull on it gently to release the cake from the pan or to invert it on a serving platter. For pans without liners, loosen the cake from the pan by sliding a warm knife or flexible metal spatula between the cake and pan, or wrap a warm wet towel around the outside of the pan for a few seconds to soften ice cream slightly. Unhinge the spring on a springform pan and remove the side of the pan. Leave the cake on its metal base to cut and serve, or carefully lift the entire cake off the metal base with a large spatula and transfer it to a serving plate. If ice cream cake is in a regular cake pan, set the bottom of the pan into lukewarm water for a few seconds and then invert cake onto a serving plate, removing any plastic or foil. Some cakes should be returned to the freezer after removing the pan to allow cake to firm up before serving.

Cut an ice cream cake: For best results, let the cake soften slightly before cutting it. Warm a sharp knife in hot water and use firm downward pressure to cut through the cake. Rinse and dry the knife between slices. To prevent melting when cutting multiple pieces, plate each slice and set the individual plates in the freezer until just before serving.

Store leftovers: After slicing and serving an ice cream cake, re-wrap remaining cake and return it to the freezer immediately. If preferred, cut and wrap individual pieces for freezing. To make a fun snack, mash leftover cake with a little milk until mushy, spoon mixture into small paper cups, add a stick to each cup and freeze the cake popsicles until solid.

Additional Tips for Successful Ice Cream Cakes

- Choose a cake recipe or mix without butter. (Butter hardens when cake is cold, making it more difficult to cut and eat.) Sponge, chiffon and other cakes made with oil work well, as do angel food cakes.

- If cake layers need to be split into thin layers, it may be easier to freeze the prepared cake before slicing. Mark your cutting line with toothpicks around the edges in order to cut straight, even layers. Angel food cakes cut easily without freezing, but use a serrated knife.

- Rich, premium ice creams soften quickly and may be easier to spread smoothly than less expensive brands.

- Chill serving plates before assembling a cake to reduce melting.

- To speed up the assembly of some layered cakes, place the individual layers (cake and/or ice cream) into plastic-lined pans and freeze the layers separately. When layers are firm, remove them from the pans, peel off the plastic and assemble or stack as directed. Frost the entire cake and return it to the freezer to set up before serving.

- Large cakes, such as those made in 9 x 13″ pans, may be cut and served directly out of the pan. If you wish to remove the cake from the pan before serving, line the pan with foil before beginning and leave some foil hanging over two opposite edges. Lift the frozen cake out of the pan using the liner, or invert cake onto a serving plate.

- Use an offset icing spatula, flexible spatula or the back of a large spoon to spread softened ice cream in smooth, even layers.

- To keep serving plates clean while frosting a cake, place strips of waxed paper under the edges of the cake before applying frosting. After freezing, remove waxed paper, leaving a clean plate.

- Use leftover cake (trimmed or removed during ice cream cake assembly) to make cake balls as directed on page 7.

Ice Cream Equivalents

1 pint	= 2 cups	
1 quart	= 4 cups	
2 quarts	= ½ gallon	= 8 cups
4 quarts	= 1 gallon	= 16 cups

Pan Size Guide

To use a different pan than directed in a recipe, be sure it will hold the correct quantity of ice cream and other ingredients. Since ice cream cakes are not baked in the pan, they can be filled almost to the rim with ingredients. Use these tips for successful substitutions.

4-cup capacity	8˝ round cake pan or 3⅝ x 7¾˝ loaf pan
6-cup capacity	9˝ round cake pan, 3⅝ x 8½˝ loaf pan or 7½˝ Bundt pan
8-cup capacity	8˝ square pan, 8˝ springform pan, 7 x 11˝ rectangular pan or 5 x 9˝ loaf pan
10-cup capacity	9˝ square pan, 9˝ springform pan or 10 x 15˝ jelly roll pan
12-cup capacity	9 x 13˝ rectangular pan, 9½˝ to 10˝ springform pan, 9˝ tube or angel food cake pan, 10˝ Bundt pan
16-cup capacity	10˝ tube pan

Cake Balls

Use leftover cake scraps that have been trimmed or removed from a shortened cake layer to make cake balls. In a medium bowl, combine 2 cups crumbled cake scraps with 2 tablespoons each of powdered sugar and unsweetened cocoa powder. By spoonfuls, stir in 2 to 3 tablespoons French vanilla-flavored liquid coffee creamer and mix by hand to make a soft dough. Roll mixture into small balls and press a toothpick into the top of each one. Place on a baking sheet and freeze for 1 hour. Coat balls with melted chocolate or almond bark and set on waxed paper until set. Remove toothpicks before serving.

To make a single gallon of ice cream, 12 pounds of milk are needed.

Simple Fudge Crunch Ice Cream Cake

Makes 12 to 16 servings

You will need
9˝ springform pan
Waxed paper

Crust
1½ C. crisp rice cereal
½ C. chopped pecans
1 (16 oz.) can chocolate fudge frosting,
  slightly warmed

Filling
½ gal. chocolate chip, rocky road
  or moose tracks ice cream, softened

Frosting
2 C. powdered sugar
3 T. unsweetened cocoa powder
¼ C. milk
¼ C. butter, softened
1 tsp. vanilla extract

8

Garnishes

Chopped or whole pecans, shaved chocolate
chocolate sprinkles or wafers

Directions

Grease a 9″ springform pan with nonstick cooking spray; set aside. In a large bowl, stir together cereal, pecans and frosting until cereal is well coated. Press mixture in bottom and up sides of prepared pan. Place pan in freezer for 20 minutes or until crust is slightly firm.

Spread softened ice cream over crust, smoothing top and pressing out any air pockets. Cover and freeze for 1 hour or until slightly firm.

Meanwhile, prepare frosting. In a medium bowl, stir together powdered sugar and cocoa. Blend in milk, butter and vanilla, beating until smooth and creamy. Remove pan from freezer and spread frosting over ice cream. Garnish with pecans and chocolate pieces. Cover pan and return to freezer for at least 3 hours.

About 15 minutes before serving, transfer pan to refrigerator. Loosen cake from pan by running a knife around edge or wrapping a warm wet towel around pan for a few seconds. Release the side of the springform pan and carefully remove it. If desired, transfer cake to a serving plate, removing waxed paper first. Cut cake into wedges and serve immediately. Freeze leftovers.

"Always serve too much hot fudge sauce on hot fudge sundaes. It makes people overjoyed and puts them in your debt."
-Judith Olney

Cake & Coffee Ice Cream Combo

Makes 12 to 16 servings

You will need
2 (8″) round cake pans
Freezer-proof serving platter or 10″ round
  cardboard wrapped in foil

Cake
1 (18.25 oz.) pkg. yellow cake mix
Eggs, oil and water as directed on package

Filling & Frosting
2 qts. coffee or mocha ice cream
  (or flavor of choice)

Garnishes
Crushed coffee-flavored hard candies, chocolate-
  covered coffee beans or chocolate shavings

Directions

Preheat oven to 350°. Grease and flour two 8″ round cake pans; set aside. In a large mixing bowl, combine cake mix, eggs, oil and water as directed on package. Beat until well mixed. Divide the batter evenly between prepared pans and bake as directed on package. Cool cakes for 10 minutes before removing them from pans. Let layers cool completely before putting cake together.

Soften 1 quart of the ice cream. If necessary, use a serrated knife to slice off the dome of one cake. Place trimmed layer on the cake plate or cardboard round. Spread softened ice cream on top of the cake layer, spreading close to the edge. Set remaining cake layer on top of the ice cream. Freeze cake for 1 to 2 hours or until firm.

Transfer remaining quart of ice cream to a large bowl. Stir ice cream until it reaches the consistency of frosting. Frost the top and sides of the frozen cake with the creamed ice cream. Icing will set up as it is spread on the cold cake. If ice cream becomes too soft to spread, return bowl and cake to freezer for 30 minutes or until firm before frosting the rest of the cake. Freeze frosted cake for at least 2 hours to harden.

To serve, remove cake from freezer and use a warm knife to cut wedges. Garnish as desired and serve immediately. Freeze leftovers.

Flavor Variations to Try
- Red velvet cake with vanilla ice cream
- Chocolate cake with cherry-nut or mint chip ice cream
- White cake with dark chocolate ice cream

Gingersnap Toffee Bombe

Makes 6 to 8 servings

You will need
3-cup round-bottomed bowl
Plastic wrap
Small round serving platter

Crust
1¼ C. crushed gingersnap cookies
3 T. butter, melted

Filling
1 pt. vanilla ice cream, softened
½ C. milk chocolate toffee bits

Toppings
⅓ C. caramel ice cream topping, warmed
Additional toffee bits

Directions

Grease a 3-cup bowl with non-stick cooking spray; line bowl with plastic wrap and set aside. In a small bowl, stir together cookie crumbs and melted butter. Press crumb mixture into bottom and up sides of prepared bowl.

In a large bowl, stir together softened ice cream and toffee bits until well combined. Spoon mixture into crust. Cover bowl and freeze until firm, at least 2 hours.

About 10 minutes before serving, remove cake from freezer. If necessary, trim edge of crust so it is even with ice cream. Set bottom of bowl into lukewarm water for a few seconds to loosen dessert. Place serving platter over bowl and invert so ice cream rests on platter; remove plastic wrap. Cut into wedges, drizzle with caramel topping and sprinkle with additional toffee bits; serve immediately. Freeze leftovers.

"Age does not diminish the extreme disappointment of having a scoop of ice cream fall from the cone."

-Jim Fiebig

Crispy Peanut Butter-Chocolate Craving

Makes 12 to 16 servings

You will need
9½″ springform pan

Chocolate Crispies
1 C. semi-sweet chocolate chips
⅓ C. creamy peanut butter
3 C. crisp rice cereal
¼ C. chopped peanuts

Filling
1 gal. vanilla ice cream, softened
¾ C. chunky peanut butter

Topping
Aerosol whipped cream, such as
   Reddi-wip, optional

Directions

In a large saucepan over medium heat, melt together chocolate chips and creamy peanut butter until smooth. Place cereal and peanuts in a large bowl and pour chocolate mixture over, stirring until well mixed. Spread coated cereal mixture on a cookie sheet and cool until firm; break up into small pieces.

Place softened ice cream in a large bowl; add the chunky peanut butter and mix until blended. Reserve ½ cup of chocolate crispy mixture for topping. Add remaining crispy mixture to ice cream and fold in until well blended. Spread ice cream in a 9½″ springform pan, smoothing the top. Sprinkle reserved crispy mixture over the top; pat down gently. Cover and freeze until very firm, about 4 hours.

About 15 minutes before serving, transfer pan to refrigerator. Loosen cake from pan by running a knife around edge or wrapping a warm wet towel around pan for a few seconds. Release the side of the springform pan and carefully remove it. Garnish top of cake with whipped cream, if desired. Cut cake into wedges and serve immediately. Freeze leftovers.

US Presidents George Washington
and Thomas Jefferson were
ice cream fans, as was inventor and
Founding Father Benjamin Franklin.

Chocolate Pretzel Deluxe

Makes 12 to 16 servings

You will need
9″ springform pan

Crust
1¼ C. crushed pretzels
6 T. butter, cut into small pieces
¾ C. hot fudge ice cream topping, warmed

Filling
20 small chocolate-covered pretzel twists*
½ gal. vanilla ice cream

Toppings
16 small chocolate-covered pretzel twists*
¼ C. caramel ice cream topping, optional

Directions

Grease the bottom of a 9˝ springform pan with nonstick cooking spray; set aside. Place crushed pretzels in a small bowl. Add butter and cut in until crumbly. Press mixture in prepared pan; cover and freeze for at least 30 minutes. Remove pan from freezer, spread fudge topping over crust, cover and return to freezer for about 30 minutes or until firm.

Soften ice cream in a large bowl. Place 20 chocolate-covered pretzels in a food processor, cover and process until crumbly. Stir crumbled pretzels into softened ice cream until blended. Spread ice cream mixture over fudge topping on frozen crust. Arrange 16 whole chocoolate-covered pretzels around top of cake, about ½˝ from outer edge. Cover and return to freezer for 8 hours or overnight.

About 10 minutes before serving, remove cake from freezer. Loosen cake from pan by running a knife around edge of pan or wrapping a warm wet towel around pan for a few seconds. Release the side of the springform pan and carefully remove it. Cut cake into wedges, drizzle with caramel topping, if desired, and serve immediately. Freeze leftovers.

* To make your own chocolate-covered pretzels, melt 8 to 10 oz. chocolate-flavored almond bark in the microwave for 60 seconds. Stir until melted and smooth, repeating if necessary. Dip pretzels into melted chocolate until coated, remove with a fork and let excess chocolate drip back into the bowl. Place pretzels on waxed paper until set, about 15 minutes.

7-Layer Neapolitan Loaf

Makes 6 to 8 servings

You will need
1 (8″ or 9″) square cake pan
Aluminum foil
Small baking sheet

Cake
1 (9 oz.) pkg. devil's food cake mix (makes one
   9″ layer cake, such as Jiffy brand)
Eggs, oil and water as directed on package

Filling
1 qt. chocolate ice cream*
1 qt. vanilla ice cream*
1 qt. strawberry ice cream*

Frosting
1 C. butter, softened
1 T. vanilla extract
7½ C. powdered sugar
¼ to ⅓ C. half & half
Food coloring, optional
Candy sprinkles, optional

Directions

Preheat oven to 350°. Grease and flour one 8″ (or 9″) square cake pan; set aside. In a medium mixing bowl, combine cake mix, eggs, oil and water as directed on package. Beat until well mixed. Spread batter in prepared pan and bake as directed on package. Cool cake for 10 minutes before removing from pan to cool completely. Place cake in freezer until slightly firm.

Cut cake in half to make two 4 x 8″ (or 4½ x 9″) rectangles. Use a serrated knife to slice each rectangle into two thin cake layers. Wrap each layer in plastic wrap and freeze for 30 minutes.

Place a 34″ piece of foil on a baking sheet. Set one frozen cake layer in the center of foil. Open carton of chocolate ice cream. From one end, cut two slices of ice cream, ¾″ to 1″ thick; place ice cream slices over top of cake layer; trim to fit. Set a second cake layer on top of chocolate ice cream, edges even. Top with slices of vanilla ice cream and another cake layer. Place strawberry ice cream and the last layer of cake on top. Trim edges as needed, keeping the stack upright. If necessary, freeze the stack after each ice cream and cake layer. Wrap cake loaf in foil and freeze for at least 2 hours or until very firm.

Meanwhile, prepare frosting. In a medium mixing bowl, stir together butter, vanilla and powdered sugar; beat in enough half & half to reach a creamy spreading consistency. Stir in food coloring as desired.

Remove cake loaf from freezer and unwrap; frost the top and sides of loaf generously. Garnish with colored sprinkles, if desired. Return to freezer for 4 hours or overnight.

About 15 minutes before serving, transfer cake to the refrigerator. Cut loaf crosswise into 1″ slices and serve immediately. Freeze leftovers.

> * Buy the ice cream in a rectangular carton for easy slicing and assembly. Freeze leftover ice cream for another use.

Banana Split Ice Cream Cake

Makes 12 to 16 servings

You will need
9˝ springform pan

Strawberry Sauce
1¼ C. frozen strawberries
3 T. sugar
½ tsp. finely grated orange zest
1 T. orange juice or water
1 tsp. cornstarch

Filling
3 C. strawberry ice cream
1 (11.75 oz.) jar chocolate fudge topping
1 (8 oz.) can crushed pineapple, drained
3 C. vanilla ice cream
3 C. chocolate ice cream

Toppings
½ C. heavy whipping cream
1 T. powdered sugar
1 banana, sliced

Directions

To prepare strawberry sauce, combine strawberries, sugar and orange zest in a small saucepan. Blend orange juice with cornstarch and stir mixture into pan. Cook and stir over medium-high heat for 7 to 8 minutes or until thickened. Refrigerate until chilled and ready to serve cake.

To make cake, soften ice cream in the refrigerator. Spread strawberry ice cream in a 9˝ springform pan, packing it well. Spread fudge topping over ice cream. Cover and freeze for 30 minutes or until firm. In a medium bowl, stir together pineapple and vanilla ice cream. Spread pineapple mixture over fudge layer and return to freezer for 30 minutes or until firm. Spread chocolate ice cream over pineapple layer. Return cake to freezer for 3 hours or until firm.

Beat whipping cream with powdered sugar until soft peaks form; set aside. To serve, loosen cake from pan by running a knife around edge of pan or wrapping a warm wet towel around pan for a few seconds. Release the side of the springform pan and carefully remove it. Spread or pipe whipped cream on cake. Garnish with banana slices; drizzle strawberry sauce on top. Cut cake into wedges and serve immediately. Freeze leftovers.

Quick-Fix Option
Substitute purchased strawberry ice cream topping for the homemade strawberry sauce.

Chocolate & Orange Delight

Makes 12 to 15 servings

You will need
9 x 13″ baking pan

Crust
2½ C. graham cracker crumbs
6 T. sugar
6 T. butter, melted

Topping
2 C. miniature marshmallows
2 C. semi-sweet chocolate chips
2 C. evaporated milk

Filling
4 C. vanilla ice cream, softened
4 C. orange sherbet, softened

Garnish
⅔ C. chopped pecans

Directions

Grease the bottom of a 9 x 13″ baking pan with nonstick cooking spray; set aside. In a medium bowl, mix together crumbs, sugar and butter until blended. Press mixture into prepared pan. Freeze for about 1 hour.

Meanwhile, in a medium saucepan over medium heat, combine marshmallows, chocolate chips and milk; cook and stir until melted, about 2 minutes. Remove chocolate sauce from heat and cool completely.

On chilled crust, arrange alternate scoops of ice cream and sherbet; press down and smooth the top with a spoon. Pour chocolate sauce over ice cream and sherbet. Sprinkle pecans on top. Cover and freeze for at least 4 hours or overnight.

About 15 minutes before serving, transfer cake to the refrigerator. Run a knife around edge of pan to loosen cake. Cut cake into squares and serve immediately. Freeze leftovers.

Eat some ice cream in July to celebrate National Ice Cream Month! But if you want to be an average American, you'll have to consume 4 to 6 gallons of ice cream within one year.

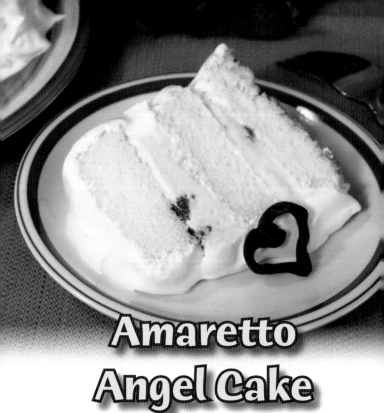

Amaretto Angel Cake

Makes 12 servings

You will need
Freezer-safe round cake platter
Aluminum foil

Cake
1 prepared round angel food cake
6 T. amaretto liqueur
1 pt. pistachio ice cream
1 pt. strawberry ice cream

Topping & Garnishes
1 C. semi-sweet chocolate chips
3 C. whipped topping
1 T. amaretto liqueur, or less to taste
Food coloring, optional

Directions

Divide the height of the angel food cake into three equal layers and mark with toothpicks. With a long serrated knife, cut the cake into three crosswise layers as marked. Separate the cake layers and sprinkle 2 tablespoons of amaretto over each layer. Place largest layer of cake on the serving platter. Cut pistachio ice cream into slices and arrange them over the first cake layer, trimming ice cream to fit. Place middle cake layer on top of the ice cream. Cut strawberry ice cream into slices and arrange them over the second cake layer, trimming to fit. Place last cake layer on top. Cover in plastic wrap and freeze for 1 hour or until firm.

Meanwhile, in a small microwave-safe bowl, melt chocolate chips, stirring until smooth. Make garnishes in one of the following ways and chill them until set. Spread chocolate on foil in a layer about ¼″ thick. Chill for 5 minutes or until almost hard. Use small cookie cutters to cut out chocolate shapes. Or, place melted chocolate in a pastry bag with a small round tip. Pipe chocolate on foil in free-form shapes (like hearts and stars) or cursive letters.

To prepare the topping, mix whipped topping with amaretto and food coloring, if desired. Frost sides and top of frozen cake, and return it to the freezer for several hours or until firm.

About 5 minutes before serving, remove cake from freezer. Arrange chocolate garnishes on cake as desired. Cut cake into wedges and serve immediately. Freeze leftovers.

To Make Raspberry Creamsicle Cake

Cut the cake into three layers as directed and spread softened vanilla ice cream between layers. Freeze overnight. Soften raspberry sherbet and stir to reach a spreading consistency. Frost frozen cake with sherbet and return to freezer. To serve, cut cake into wedges, garnish with fresh raspberries or raspberry sauce and serve immediately.

Layered Frozen Peach Cobbler

Makes 10 to 12 servings

You will need
9˝ square baking pan
5 x 9˝ loaf pan
Plastic wrap

Cake
1 (9 oz.) pkg. white cake mix (makes one
  9˝ layer cake, such as Jiffy brand)
Eggs, oil and water as directed on package

Filling
2 C. vanilla ice cream
1 C. chopped fresh or frozen peaches
2 C. cinnamon ice cream
2 C. peach frozen yogurt or peach sorbet
Orange food coloring, optional

Cobbler & Topping

1½ C. quick oats
½ C. brown sugar
1 tsp. ground cinnamon
½ C. butter
Whipped topping, optional

Directions

Preheat oven to 350°. Grease and flour a 9˝ square baking pan; set aside. In a medium mixing bowl, combine cake mix, eggs, oil and water as directed on package. Spread batter in prepared pan and bake as directed on package. Cool cake for 10 minutes before removing from pan to cool completely.

With a serrated knife, trim cake to fit into the loaf pan; reserve leftover cake for another use. Wrap and freeze trimmed cake. Meanwhile, coat loaf pan with nonstick cooking spray and line with plastic wrap, leaving a generous overhang.

Soften vanilla ice cream in a large bowl; stir in peaches until blended. Spread mixture in prepared pan and freeze for 2 hours or until firm. Soften cinnamon ice cream. Remove pan from freezer and spread cinnamon ice cream on top of vanilla layer. Return pan to freezer for 1 hour. Soften peach yogurt and stir in orange food coloring, if desired. Spread yogurt on top of cinnamon layer. Unwrap and set chilled cake on top, pressing lightly in place. Wrap snugly with plastic overhang and freeze for at least 2 hours or until firm.

Meanwhile, prepare the cobbler. Preheat oven to 350°. In a medium bowl, stir together oats, brown sugar and cinnamon. Cut in butter until crumbly. Spread mixture in a 9˝ baking pan and bake for 15 minutes. Cool completely. Break mixture into chunks and set aside.

About 10 minutes before serving, set bottom of loaf pan into lukewarm water for a few seconds to loosen cake from pan. Lift cake out of pan using the plastic wrap. Invert on a serving plate, with white cake on the bottom; remove plastic wrap. Slice cake, sprinkle with cobbler topping and garnish with whipped topping, if desired. Serve immediately. Freeze leftovers.

Macaroon Torte

Makes 12 to 16 servings

You will need
9˝ springform pan

Torte
24 macaroon cookies, crumbled, divided
4 C. coffee-flavored ice cream, softened, divided
4 C. chocolate ice cream, softened, divided
1 C. milk chocolate toffee bits, divided

Toppings
Toasted coconut*, optional
Hot fudge topping, warmed

Directions

Press about a third of the crumbled cookies Into the bottom of an ungreased 9″ springform pan. Spread 2 cups of coffee-flavored ice cream over cookies, smoothing top. Sprinkle another third of the cookies over ice cream, pressing down lightly. Spread 2 cups of chocolate ice cream over cookies. Top with ½ cup toffee bits. Repeat the layers with remaining coffee-flavored ice cream, cookies, chocolate ice cream and toffee bits. Cover and freeze for at least 4 hours or until firm.

About 10 minutes before serving, remove cake from freezer. Loosen cake from pan by running a knife around edge of pan or wrapping a warm wet towel around pan for a few seconds. Release the side of the springform pan and carefully remove it. Sprinkle top of cake with toasted coconut, if desired. Cut cake into wedges, drizzle with hot fudge topping and serve immediately. Freeze leftovers.

* To toast, place ½ cup sweetened flaked coconut in a skillet and toss over medium heat until golden brown; let cool.

"My advice to you is not to inquire why or whither, but just enjoy your ice cream while it's on your plate."
—Thornton Niven Wilder

Tic-Tac-Toe Fun

Makes 10 to 12 servings

You will need
10˝ springform pan

Crust
3 C. finely crushed chocolate cream-filled
   sandwich cookies
½ C. sugar
½ C. butter, melted

Filling
5 C. vanilla ice cream, softened
4 C. chocolate ice cream, softened

Ganache
1 C. semi-sweet chocolate chips
½ C. heavy whipping cream

Garnish
Miniature Oreo cookies, optional

Directions

In a large bowl, stir together crushed cookies, sugar and butter; set aside ½ cup for the topping. Press remaining cookie mixture on the bottom and about 1½″ up the sides of an ungreased 10″ springform pan.

By tablespoonfuls, place 1¾ cups vanilla ice cream on top of crust around edge of pan. Flatten and smooth ice cream into a ring about 1½″ wide. Using the same method, place and spread 1 cup of chocolate ice cream into a 1½″-wide ring next to the vanilla ring. Fill in the center space with ¼ cup vanilla ice cream. Freeze for at least 30 minutes.

For the second ice cream layer, reverse the pattern, placing 1¾ cups chocolate ice cream in the outer ring over vanilla ice cream, followed by 1 cup of vanilla ice cream in the middle ring over chocolate ice cream. Fill in the center with ¼ cup chocolate ice cream over vanilla ice cream. Freeze for at least 30 minutes.

For the third ice cream layer, repeat the pattern of the first layer. Sprinkle reserved crumb mixture over the top. Cover and freeze at least 4 hours or until firm.

About 20 minutes before serving, make ganache. Place chocolate chips in a medium heat-proof bowl and set aside. In a small saucepan, heat cream to near boiling. Pour hot cream over chocolate and let stand for 2 to 3 minutes until melted. Stir until smooth. Ten minutes before serving, remove ice cream cake from the freezer. Loosen cake from pan by running a knife around edge of pan or wrapping a warm wet towel around pan for a few seconds. Release the side of the springform pan and carefully remove it. Cut cake into wedges. Drizzle with ganache, garnish with optional cookies and serve immediately. Freeze leftovers.

Raspberry Ribbon Beauty

Makes 12 to 16 servings

You will need
9″ to 9½″ springform pan

Crust
1½ C. crushed shortbread cookies or
   chocolate wafers
¼ C. butter, melted

Sauce
2 C. fresh or frozen raspberries
½ C. light corn syrup
⅓ C. sugar
⅓ C. water

Filling & Garnish
6 to 8 C. vanilla ice cream, divided
½ C. sliced almonds

Directions

Grease a 9″ or 9½″ springform pan with nonstick cooking spray; set aside. In a small bowl, combine crushed cookies and melted butter; press into the bottom of prepared pan. Cover and freeze for 1 hour or until firm.

In a medium saucepan over medium heat, combine raspberries, corn syrup, sugar and water. Bring to a boil and cook for 10 minutes. Let cool slightly. Transfer mixture to a blender, cover and puree until smooth. Pour into a bowl and refrigerate for 30 minutes or until cool, stirring occasionally.

Remove crust from freezer. Soften half of the ice cream and spread it on crust. Reserve ¼ cup of raspberry sauce; pour remaining sauce over ice cream. Cover and return to freezer for 2 hours or until firm.

Soften remaining ice cream. Remove dessert from freezer and spread ice cream over raspberry sauce. Cover with plastic wrap and freeze for 6 hours or overnight.

About 15 minutes before serving, remove cake from freezer. Loosen cake from pan by running a knife around edge of pan or wrapping a warm wet towel around pan for a few seconds. Release the side of the springform pan and carefully remove it. Drizzle reserved raspberry sauce over dessert and sprinkle with almonds. Cut cake into wedges and serve immediately. Freeze leftovers.

Quick-Fix Option
Substitute seedless raspberry jam for the homemade raspberry sauce, warming slightly for easy spreading.

Mexican Crunch Ice Cream Cake

Makes 12 to 16 servings

You will need
9˝ springform pan

Crust
1 C. cornflake crumbs
⅓ C. sugar
⅓ C. butter, melted
¾ tsp. ground cinnamon

Filling & Topping
½ gal. butter pecan ice cream, divided
4 T. honey, divided

Directions

Grease a 9″ springform pan with nonstick cooking spray; set aside. In a small bowl, combine cornflake crumbs, sugar, butter and cinnamon until well blended. Reserve ½ cup of crumb mixture; press remaining crumbs into the bottom of prepared pan. Soften half of the ice cream; spoon softened ice cream over crust, pressing down well. Sprinkle reserved crumb mixture over ice cream. Drizzle with 2 tablespoons honey. Cover and freeze for at least 2 hours.

Soften remaining ice cream. Remove pan from freezer and spread softened ice cream over the top. Cover and return to freezer for 8 hours or overnight.

About 10 minutes before serving, remove cake from freezer. Loosen cake from pan by running a knife around edge of pan or wrapping a warm wet towel around pan for a few seconds. Release the side of the springform pan and carefully remove it. Drizzle top of cake with remaining 2 tablespoons honey. Cut cake into wedges and serve immediately. Freeze leftovers.

In the United States, the most popular ice cream flavor is vanilla followed by chocolate. Other favorites are neapolitan, strawberry, cookies 'n cream, butter brickle and mint chocolate chip. The most popular ice cream topping is chocolate sauce.

Strawberry Jelly Roll Swirl

Makes 8 to 10 servings

You will need
10½ x 15½″ jelly roll pan
Tea towel and powdered sugar
2- to 2½-quart bowl
Plastic wrap
Round serving platter

Jelly Roll Cake
½ C. all-purpose flour
¼ tsp. baking powder
¼ tsp. salt
3 large eggs
½ C. sugar
1 tsp. vanilla extract
2 T. vegetable oil
1 C. strawberry or raspberry jam

Fillings
1 (4 oz.) dark chocolate baking bar,
  broken into pieces
¼ C. heavy whipping cream
3 to 4 C. strawberry or raspberry ice cream

Garnishes
Whipped topping
Fresh strawberries or raspberries

Directions
Preheat oven to 350°. Grease a 10½ x 15½″ jelly roll pan with nonstick cooking spray. Line bottom with waxed paper and spray again; set aside. In a small bowl, combine flour, baking powder and salt; set aside. In a large mixing bowl, beat eggs, sugar and vanilla for 5 to 10 minutes or until thick and pale yellow. Beat in oil and flour mixture. Spread batter in prepared pan and bake for 13 to 16 minutes or until lightly browned. Sprinkle a tea towel generously with powdered sugar. Immediately invert cake onto towel and peel off waxed paper. Starting at a long side, roll up warm cake with towel inside. Place seam-side down on a wire rack to cool completely.

Unroll cake and remove towel. Spread jam over cake to within ½″ of edges. Re-roll cake, cover with plastic wrap and freeze for at least 2 hours.

To prepare chocolate filling, combine chocolate pieces and cream in a small microwave-safe bowl. Cook on high for 30 seconds. Stir and repeat until melted and smooth. Cool completely.

With a serrated knife, cut frozen jelly roll into ⅜″ slices. Coat a 2-quart bowl with nonstick cooking spray and line it with plastic wrap. Tightly line bottom and sides of bowl with cake slices to create a mold; freeze for 30 minutes. Soften strawberry ice cream slightly; spoon 1 to 1½ cups of ice cream into mold and freeze again. Remove bowl from freezer and spread chocolate filling over ice cream; freeze for at least 1 hour. Remove bowl from freezer and spread remaining ice cream over chocolate, filling cake mold completely. Cover and freeze for 3 hours or until firm.

About 15 minutes before serving, remove bowl from freezer and dip bottom of bowl into lukewarm water for a few seconds. Invert bowl onto a serving platter and peel off plastic wrap. Garnish with whipped topping and berries. Cut into wedges and serve immediately. Freeze leftovers.

Mint Chip Chocolate Stack

Makes 10 to 12 servings

You will need
9˝ springform pan

Crust & Topping
2 C. crushed chocolate wafer cookies or
  chocolate sandwich cookies, divided
¼ C. margarine, melted

Filling
7 C. mint chip ice cream, divided
2½ to 3 C. chocolate chip or chocolate chip cookie
  dough ice cream

Directions

Grease an 8″ or 9″ springform pan with nonstick cooking spray; set aside. Reserve ½ cup crushed cookies for topping. In a medium bowl, combine remaining crushed cookies with melted margarine until well blended. Press mixture into the bottom of prepared pan and freeze for at least 1 hour.

Soften half of the mint chip ice cream slightly. Spread over cookie crust, packing it down well. Freeze for 2 hours or until firm.

Soften chocolate chip ice cream slightly. Spread over mint chip ice cream and return to freezer for 2 hours or until firm.

Soften remaining mint chip ice cream and spread over chocolate chip ice cream. Sprinkle reserved crushed cookies over the top of cake and freeze for at least 4 hours or until very firm.

About 15 minutes before serving, remove cake from freezer. Loosen cake from pan by running a knife around edge of pan or wrapping a warm wet towel around pan for a few seconds. Release the side of the springform pan and carefully remove it. Cut cake into wedges and serve immediately. Freeze leftovers.

This ice cream cake can also be made in a 9 x 13″ baking pan, but make crust with 2¼ cups of cookie crumbs and 6 tablespoons margarine. To serve, simply cut cake into squares and serve out of the pan.

Giant Brownie Ice Cream Sandwich

Makes 9 to 12 servings

You will need
2 (8˝) square baking pans
Aluminum foil
Baking sheet or freezer-proof serving platter

Crust
1 (19 to 22 oz.) pkg. brownie mix
Eggs, oil and water as directed on package
1 C. chopped Milky Way candy bars

Filling
1 qt. vanilla or mint chip ice cream*

Toppings
1½ C. whipped topping
1 C. candy-coated chocolate candies

Directions

Preheat oven to 350°. Grease two 8˝ square baking pans with nonstick cooking spray and line with foil, leaving an overhang on opposite sides. Spray foil generously with nonstick cooking spray and set aside. In a large bowl, combine brownie mix, eggs, oil and water as directed on package for fudge-like brownies. Stir in candy bars until blended. Divide the batter evenly between prepared pans and bake as directed on package, about 25 minutes. Cool brownies completely in pans. Cover pans in plastic wrap and freeze both pans for at least 1 hour.

Lift foil to remove brownies from pans; peel off foil. Invert one frozen brownie onto a baking sheet or serving platter. Cut ice cream into 1˝ thick slices and cover brownie with ice cream slices, placing edges even. Set remaining frozen brownie on top of ice cream with all edges even; press gently in place. With an offset spatula, smooth edges of ice cream as needed. Spread whipped topping on top of brownie. Freeze for 2 hours or until firm.

About 15 minutes before serving, remove cake from freezer. Sprinkle candies on slightly softened whipped topping, pressing in place as needed. Cut cake into pieces and serve immediately. Freeze leftovers.

> * Buy the ice cream in a rectangular carton for easy slicing and assembly. Freeze leftover ice cream for another use.

Chocolate Chunk Ice Cream Squares

Makes 12 to 14 servings

You will need
7 x 10½ x 3˝ plastic storage container
   or baking dish
Plastic wrap
Waxed paper
Freezer-safe serving platter

Cake & Filling
4 C. caramel ice cream, softened
3 C. coarsely crushed frozen Twix cookie
   bars, divided
3 T. butter, melted
4 C. chocolate ice cream
1 (10.75 oz.) frozen butter pound cake

Topping
1 C. milk chocolate or dark chocolate chips
½ C. heavy whipping cream

Directions

Grease a 7 x 10½ x 3˝ plastic storage container or baking dish with nonstick cooking spray; line with plastic wrap and set aside. Soften the caramel ice cream. Spread ice cream over the bottom of prepared pan. Sprinkle half of the crushed cookie bars over ice cream. Freeze for 1 hour or until firm.

In a small bowl, combine remaining crushed cookie bars with melted butter; set aside. Soften the chocolate ice cream. Spread chocolate ice cream over crushed cookies in pan. Sprinkle cookie mixture over chocolate ice cream. Cut pound cake into 12 to 14 equal slices and arrange slices on top of cookie mixture, pressing lightly in place. Cover and freeze for 3 hours or until firm.

About 20 minutes before serving, prepare chocolate topping. Place chocolate chips in a medium heat-proof bowl and set aside. In a small saucepan, heat cream to near boiling. Pour hot cream over chocolate and let stand for 2 to 3 minutes until melted. Stir until smooth; let cool slightly. Remove cake from freezer and set bottom of pan into lukewarm water for a few seconds to loosen. Invert pan on a large serving platter and remove cake from pan. Peel off plastic wrap. Drizzle chocolate topping over the top and sides of the whole cake before cutting, or cut cake into pieces and drizzle topping over each piece just before serving. Serve immediately. Freeze leftovers.

"Without ice cream, life and fame are meaningless."
-Unknown

Sherbet & Ice Cream Party Cake

Makes 14 to 16 servings

You will need
10˝ tube pan
Aluminum foil
3 baking sheets
Waxed paper
Freezer-safe serving plate

Filling
3 C. raspberry sherbet
3 C. orange sherbet
3 C. lime sherbet
3 qts. vanilla ice cream, divided
1½ C. miniature semi-sweet chocolate chips,
   divided

Toppings
Aerosol whipped cream, such as
   Reddi-wip, optional
Fresh raspberries, optional

Directions

If using a two-piece angel food cake pan, wrap foil around the bottom of the pan to prevent leaking. Line three baking sheets with waxed paper; set aside. Shape sherbet into balls with a ¼-cup ice cream scoop, making 11 to 12 of each flavor. Place them on prepared baking sheets and freeze for 1 hour or until firm.

Soften 1 quart of vanilla ice cream. In a large bowl, combine softened ice cream and ¾ cup chocolate chips until well mixed. Spread mixture in prepared tube pan, packing well. Arrange 3 to 4 sherbet balls of each color alternately on ice cream, placing them against the center tube and outer edge of pan. Place in freezer for 30 minutes.

Soften another quart of vanilla ice cream and spread it over sherbet; freeze for 30 minutes. Remove pan from freezer and place remaining sherbet balls on top of ice cream. Soften last quart of ice cream and stir in remaining ¾ cup chocolate chips. Spread over sherbet balls. Cover and freeze for 6 hours or overnight.

To remove cake from pan, wrap outside of pan with a warm wet towel for 20 to 30 seconds. Run a knife around edge and center tube of pan to loosen cake and invert cake onto a serving plate. Remove pan and return cake to freezer until firm.

About 10 minutes before serving, remove cake from freezer. Garnish top with dollops of whipped cream and fresh berries, if desired. Cut cake into wedges and serve immediately. Freeze leftovers.

"Not to like ice cream is to show oneself uninterested in food."
-Joseph Epstein

Frozen Black Forest Elegance

Makes 12 to 14 servings

You will need
3 (9˝) round cake pans

Filling
1 qt. cherry or cherry-chocolate ice cream,
  softened

Cake
1¾ C. all-purpose flour
2 C. sugar
¾ C. unsweetened cocoa powder
2 tsp. baking soda
1 tsp. baking powder
1 tsp. salt
2 eggs
¾ C. brewed coffee, cooled
1 C. buttermilk or sour milk
½ C. vegetable oil
1 tsp. vanilla extract

Toppings
1 (12 oz.) carton whipped topping, thawed
1 C. cherry pie filling

Directions
Line one 9″ round cake pan with aluminum foil. Pack ice cream firmly into foil-lined pan, pressing the top smooth. Cover and freeze for about 2 hours.

Generously grease and flour two 9″ round cake pans; set aside. Preheat oven to 350°. In a large mixing bowl, whisk together flour, sugar, cocoa powder, baking soda, baking powder and salt. Add eggs, coffee, buttermilk, oil and vanilla; beat on medium speed for 2 minutes. Pour batter into prepared baking pans. Bake for 30 minutes or until a toothpick comes out clean. Cool cakes for 15 minutes before removing from pans to cool completely.

Invert one cake layer onto a serving plate. Remove the frozen ice cream disk from its pan, place it upside down on the cake and remove foil. Place second cake layer, top side up, over ice cream. Spread whipped topping over top and sides of cake. Pipe or spoon more whipped topping around the top edge of cake to make a well in the center. Cover and freeze cake for at least 3 hours or overnight.

About 10 minutes before serving, remove cake from freezer. Spoon cherry pie filling into the whipped topping well on the top of cake. Cut cake into wedges and serve immediately. Freeze leftovers.

Quick-Fix Option
Use a chocolate cake mix (9 x 13″ size) and prepare with eggs, oil and water as directed on package. Bake as directed for two 9″ pans. Omit whipped topping well on cake top, but after cutting cake into wedges, spoon some cherry pie filling over each piece.

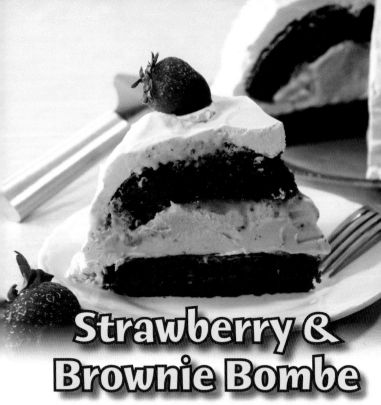

Strawberry & Brownie Bombe

Makes 12 to 16 servings

You will need
2 (8″) round baking pans
1½-qt. bowl with rounded bottom
Aluminum foil
Freezer-safe serving plate
Pastry bag with star tip, optional

Brownie
1 (18 to 22 oz.) pkg. fudge brownie mix
  (9 x 13″ size)
Eggs, oil and water as directed on package
⅓ C. chopped walnuts

Filling
½ C. strawberry preserves
1 qt. strawberry ice cream

Garnishes
Fresh whole strawberries
Milk chocolate candy wafers, melted

Frosting

2 C. heavy whipping cream
Red food coloring, optional
¼ C. powdered sugar

Directions

Grease two 8˝ round baking pans and line the bottoms with waxed paper; set aside. Chill a medium mixing bowl and beaters in the freezer. Preheat oven to 350°. In a large mixing bowl, combine brownie mix, eggs, oil and water as directed on package for cake-like brownies. Stir in walnuts. Divide batter between prepared pans and bake for 30 minutes or until a toothpick comes out clean. Cool completely in pans.

Line a 1½-quart bowl with foil. Remove brownie rounds from pans and peel off waxed paper. Gently press one brownie into the bowl with top of brownie against foil. (Brownie may crack slightly.) Spread preserves over brownie. Freeze for 15 to 30 minutes.

Soften ice cream. Fill brownie-lined bowl with ice cream, smoothing the top. Cover and freeze for at least 3 hours or until ice cream is firm.

Place remaining brownie on a serving plate. Remove bowl from freezer, uncover, and invert onto brownie on plate, ice cream side down. Remove bowl and foil; return to freezer.

Dip strawberries into melted chocolate and place on waxed paper until set. In the chilled mixing bowl, beat whipping cream and food coloring until soft peaks form. Add powdered sugar and beat until almost stiff peaks form. Place 1½ cups of whipped cream into a pastry bag with a star tip, set aside. Remove cake from freezer and spread remaining whipped cream over top and sides of cake. Pipe whipped cream around base of cake; refrigerate pastry bag with remaining whipped cream. Freeze cake for 1 to 2 hours or until firm.

About 10 minutes before serving, remove cake from freezer. Pipe whipped cream on top of cake and garnish with chocolate strawberries. Slice cake into wedges and serve immediately. Freeze leftovers.

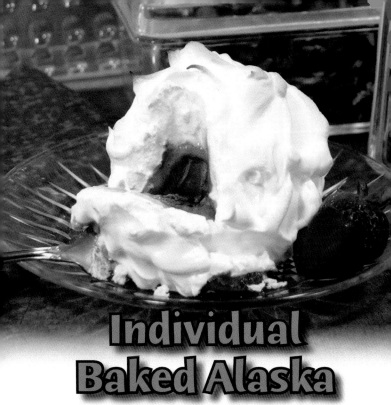

Individual Baked Alaska

Makes 6 to 8 servings

You will need
Large baking pan
Broiler pan
Aluminum foil

Crust
6 to 8 baked or purchased 3˝ sugar cookies

Filling
½ gal. chocolate-almond or chocolate revel
  ice cream

Meringue
5 large egg whites, room temperature
¼ tsp. cream of tartar
¾ C. sugar

Directions

Prepare your favorite cookie dough or use refrigerated cookie dough to bake 3″ round cookies, or use purchased cookies.

Place cookies on a baking pan. Place a large scoop* of ice cream on top of each cookie, pressing down to hold it in place. Freeze ice cream cookies on baking pan for at least 1 hour or until ice cream is very hard.

Before serving, prepare the meringue. In a large mixing bowl, beat egg whites on medium speed until frothy. Add cream of tartar, increase speed and beat until soft peaks form. Add sugar, 1 tablespoon at a time, and continue to beat until stiff peaks form.

Preheat oven to 500°. Remove ice cream cookies from the freezer and transfer to a broiler pan. Using a spoon, quickly spread the meringue evenly over the ice cream, covering it completely and attaching meringue to edge of cookies. Place pan in the hot oven and bake just until meringue is lightly browned, about 2 minutes.

Remove pan from oven, transfer desserts to individual plates and serve immediately.

* If a large ice cream scoop is not available, line a punch cup or similar mold with plastic wrap and press ice cream into cup; pull out plastic to unmold the ice cream ball.

Flavor Variations to Try

Choose any cookie and ice cream flavors you enjoy, such as chocolate-macadamia nut cookies with strawberry or cherry ice cream, chocolate chip cookies with vanilla ice cream, snickerdoodle cookies with caramel ice cream or sugar cookies with mint chip ice cream.

Chocolate Peppermint Cake Roll

Makes 10 servings

You will need
10½ x 15½ x 1″ jelly roll pan
Waxed paper
Tea towel and powdered sugar
Aluminum foil

Cake
⅓ C. all-purpose flour
¼ C. unsweetened cocoa powder
1 tsp. baking powder
½ tsp. salt
4 eggs, separated, room temperature
½ tsp. vanilla extract
⅓ C. plus ½ C. sugar, divided
¼ tsp. cream of tartar
Powdered sugar

Filling
1 qt. peppermint or mint chip ice cream

Frosting & Garnish

4 oz. unsweetened chocolate, chopped
¼ C. butter
4 C. powdered sugar
⅓ C. plus 1 to 3 T. milk, divided
Crushed peppermint candy or candy canes

Directions

Preheat oven to 375°. Grease a 10½ x 15½" jelly roll pan and line with waxed paper. Grease and flour the waxed paper; set aside. In a small bowl, whisk together flour, cocoa powder, baking powder and salt; set aside. In a medium mixing bowl, beat together egg yolks and vanilla for 5 minutes or until thick. Gradually beat in ⅓ cup sugar; set aside.

Wash beaters well. In a large mixing bowl, beat egg whites until frothy. Add cream of tartar and beat until soft peaks form. Gradually beat in remaining ½ cup sugar until stiff peaks form. Fold egg yolk mixture into stiff egg whites. Gently fold in flour mixture. Spread batter in prepared pan. Bake for 12 to 15 minutes or until cake springs back when touched.

Sprinkle a tea towel generously with powdered sugar. Loosen edges of cake with a knife and immediately invert cake onto towel; peel off waxed paper. Starting from a short end, roll up warm cake with towel inside. Place seam-side down on a wire rack to cool completely.

Soften ice cream. Unroll cake and remove towel. Spread ice cream on cake to within 1" of the edges. Re-roll cake and wrap in foil. Freeze for 6 hours.

To prepare frosting, combine chocolate and butter in a small saucepan over low heat until melted. Remove from heat; stir in powdered sugar and ⅓ cup milk until smooth. Stir in remaining remaining milk to reach a smooth spreading consistency.

Remove cake from freezer and spread chocolate frosting over entire roll, working quickly. Sprinkle with crushed candies. Cover and freeze for at least 2 hours.

About 10 minutes before serving, remove cake from freezer. Slice cake roll into 1" slices and serve immediately. Freeze leftovers.

Lemon Tunnel Surprise

Makes 12 servings

You will need
10″ fluted tube or Bundt pan

Cake
1 (18.25 oz.) pkg. lemon cake mix
Eggs, oil and water as directed on package

Filling
2 C. lemon sherbet or sorbet
2 C. key lime pie frozen yogurt or lime sherbet

Frosting
1 C. ready-to-spread cream cheese frosting
1 to 2 tsp. lemon juice
¾ tsp. finely grated lemon zest

Directions

Preheat oven to 350°. Thoroughly grease and flour a 10″ fluted tube pan; set aside. In a large mixing bowl, combine cake mix, eggs, oil and water as directed on package. Pour batter into prepared pan and bake for 35 to 40 minutes or until a toothpick comes out clean. Cool cake for 10 minutes before removing from pan to cool completely.

Using a long serrated knife, slice off the top fourth of the cake; set aside. With a smaller knife, carefully hollow out and remove the center portion of the bottom of cake, leaving a ½″ to ¾″ shell. Reserve removed cake for another use. Freeze cake shell for 1 hour.

Soften sherbet slightly. Remove cake shell from freezer and spoon lemon sherbet into the tunnel in cake, packing it lightly and smoothing top. Spoon lime frozen yogurt on top to make a second layer, filling tunnel. Replace top of cake, lining up edges. Cover and freeze for at least 6 hours.

About 10 minutes before serving, remove cake from freezer. In a small microwave-safe bowl, stir together frosting, lemon juice and zest. Heat in microwave for 15 seconds or until slightly warmed; stir until it reaches a drizzling consistency. Drizzle over cake. Slice cake into wedges and serve immediately. Freeze leftovers.

To Make Coconut Tunnel Surprise

Mix 1 to 2 cups vanilla ice cream and 1 teaspoon coconut flavoring, or purchase coconut gelato to use in place of the key lime yogurt. Assemble cake as directed and sprinkle toasted coconut on top.

Quick & Elegant Ice Cream Sandwich Torte

Makes 10 to 12 servings

You will need
Aluminum foil
Small baking sheet

Layers & Frosting
½ C. hot fudge ice cream topping, warmed
1 to 2 T. milk, optional
1 (8 oz.) carton whipped topping, thawed, divided
1 (3.9 oz.) pkg. instant chocolate pudding mix
8 chocolate cream-filled sandwich cookies
  or chocolate wafers, chopped
1 C. chocolate-covered peanuts, chopped

Crust & Filling
12 vanilla ice cream sandwiches, unwrapped

Directions

Pour fudge topping into a medium bowl; thin with a little milk if needed. Add 1 cup whipped topping and whisk together until well blended. Add dry pudding mix and stir for 2 minutes or until smooth and well blended. Gently stir in cookies and peanuts, set aside.

Place a 24″ piece of foil on a baking sheet. Arrange four of the ice cream sandwiches down the center of the foil, placing them next to each other with long sides touching. Spread half of the pudding mixture over the sandwiches. Set four more ice cream sandwiches on top and spread remaining pudding mixture over the sandwiches. Top with remaining four ice cream sandwiches.

Frost top and sides of ice cream cake with remaining whipped topping. Wrap foil around cake, sealing loosely, and freeze on baking sheet for at least 4 hours or until firm.

About 10 minutes before serving, remove cake from freezer to soften slightly. Cut loaf crosswise into slices about ¾″ wide and serve immediately. Freeze leftovers.

Ice cream should be stored in a freezer at temperatures between -5° and 0° F. But don't serve it quite that cold! The ideal serving temperature is 6° to 10° F.

Pumpkin-Chip S'mores

Makes 12 to 16 servings

You will need
9″ springform pan
Butane torch or lighter

Crust
9 whole chocolate graham cracker rectangles
6 T. butter, cut into small pieces

Filling
3½ pts. pumpkin ice cream*
1 C. dark chocolate chips, chopped
1 (7½ oz.) jar marshmallow creme
1 (10½ oz.) bag miniature marshmallows,
   divided

Directions

Grease the bottom of a 9″ springform pan with nonstick cooking spray; set aside. In a food processor, combine graham crackers and butter; process until crumbs form moist clumps. Press cracker mixture into the bottom of prepared pan and freeze for 1 hour.

Soften ice cream in a large bowl. Stir in chopped chocolate. Spread ice cream over crust and freeze for 2 hours. In a medium bowl, stir together marshmallow creme and half of the marshmallows; spread marshmallow mixture over ice cream layer. Sprinkle remaining marshmallows on top, pressing down in place. Cover and freeze at least 24 hours.

About 10 minutes before serving, remove cake from freezer. Loosen cake from pan by running a knife around edge of pan or wrapping a warm wet towel around pan for a few seconds. Release the side of the springform pan and carefully remove it. Transfer cake to a serving plate. With a butane torch, carefully toast marshmallows on top of cake until light golden brown. Cut cake into wedges and serve immediately. Freeze leftovers.

* Make your own pumpkin ice cream in any season. In a large bowl, combine 1½ quarts softened vanilla ice cream, ¾ cup pumpkin puree, 6 tablespoons brown sugar and ¼ teaspoon each of ground ginger, ground cinnamon and ground nutmeg; stir until well blended.

"I scream, you scream, we all scream for ice cream."
-Johnson, Moll and King

Tasty Combos

Put different layers together, freezing after each layer is added.

- Cake + ice cream + cake + ice cream + cake + frosting in round or loaf pans

- Ice cream flavor #1 + ice cream flavor #2 + ice cream flavor #3 in springform pans or domed bowls to make bombes

- Crunchy crust + ice cream + crunchy middle layer + ice cream + crunchy topping in any pan

- Cake + sauce + ice cream + cake + ice cream + sauce topping in any pan

Dress up softened ice cream with an array of mix-ins.
Stir crushed cookies, candies, sprinkles, chocolate chips, or chunks of cookie dough into softened ice cream of your choice before assembling the cake.

Use interesting crusts and sprinkles.
Crush ingredients like cookies, pretzels, crackers or cereal and combine them with melted butter and sugar to create a crust. Press the crust into the bottom of a pan and reserve some of the plain crushed ingredients to garnish the top of the cake.

Try different frostings.
- Spread the top and/or sides of ice cream cake with sweetened whipped cream, whipped topping, whipped cream icing, fudge ganache, buttercream frosting or cream cheese frosting. This can be done before freezing or just before serving.

- Meringue makes a nice topping but must be applied and broiled or baked at 500° just before serving.

Add great garnishes.
- Dip pieces of fresh fruit into white or dark chocolate and place on top of the cake just before serving.

- Drizzle syrups and sauces on top of the whole cake, individual plated pieces or the empty plate before setting the wedge of cake on it. Try flavors such as raspberry, strawberry, chocolate fudge or caramel.

- Sprinkle crushed candies or cookies over the cake or set whole ones on edge.